201 WAYS TO GET EVEN WITH YOUR BOSS

201 WAYS TO GET EVEN WITH YOUR BOSS

by

LINDA HIGGINS

A Citadel Press Book
Published by Carol Publishing Group

A Citadel Press Book
Published by Carol Publishing Group
Citadel Press is a registered trademark of Carol Communications, Inc.
Editorial Offices: 600 Madison Avenue, New York, N.Y. 10022
Sales & Distribution Offices: 120 Enterprise Avenue, Secaucus, N.J. 07094
In Canada: Canadian Manda Group, P.O. Box 920, Station U, Toronto, Ontario M8Z 5P9
Queries regarding rights and permissions should be addressed to Carol Publishing Group, 600 Madison Avenue, New York, N.Y. 10022

Carol Publishing Group books are available at special discounts for bulk purchases, sales promotions, fund-raising, or educational purposes.
Special editions can be created to specifications.
For details contact: Special Sales Department, Carol Publishing Group, 120 Enterprise Avenue, Secaucus, N.J. 07094

Manufactured in the United States of America
10 9 8 7 6 5 4 3 2 1

Library of Congress Cataloging-in-Publication Data

Higgins, Linda.
    201 ways to get even with your boss / by Linda Higgins.
        p.   cm.
    "A Citadel Press book."
    ISBN 0-8065-1570-8
    1. Supervisors—Humor. I. Title. II. Title: Two hundred one ways to get even with your boss. III. Title: Two hundred and one ways to get even with your boss.
PN6162.H485   1994
818'.5402–dc20   94-20518
                                                                            CIP

ACKNOWLEDGMENTS

I would like to thank the following people for helping make this book possible: Steve Schragis, who decided to publish the book; Bill Birnes, my agent; Eileen Cotton and Jim Ellison, my editors; Tim Ballou, my writing partner on other books, which hopefully you will be reading in the future; Pam Kirsh Leon and Carol Fein Ross, for their legal expertise; and my mother, Pauline, for her endless prayers.

DEDICATION

I dedicate this book in loving memory to my father, Gregory. My father was a man who knew how to laugh, and he also knew the importance of owning your own business, thus eliminating the need for a boss.

DISCLAIMER

This book is in no way a reflection on any of the individuals with whom I have had the pleasure of working.

This book is intended as a joke. The writer and publisher shall in no instance be held accountable for any litigation resulting from any individual's use of the material in this book.

INTRODUCTION

Your boss calls you into his office at five P.M. and presents you with an enormous project that must be ready by nine A.M. the following morning. He bellows that it is of the utmost importance and he doesn't care if you have to stay at work until two A.M. to finish it. You work until four A.M. and show up at nine A.M. with project in hand, imagining you'll hear "What a great job!" or "I knew I could count on you!" Instead you hear your boss is on vacation. He flew to New York last night.

Your boss claims it is not part of his job to carry an overhead slide projector, screen, and several heavy boxes of display equipment out to his car. Rather than ask the sixty-one-year-old receptionist to do it, as your six-foot-four-inch boss suggests, you make several trips out to the parking lot hauling equipment that would have taken your boss one trip. As you stagger back to the office out of breath from this laborious task, instead of hearing "Thank you," you get yelled at because you haven't finished typing the letter you started before you became a teamster.

Now you no longer have to daydream about how to plot your revenge against a nincompoop of a boss. This book shows you in detail how to say "Thank you" for all those rude and inconsiderate gestures you have received over the years.

Not all of the suggestions are for everyone. Take the test on the next few pages, rate your boss, and let your score determine which pranks to play. Some are in the "fun-loving" category, and these selections are denoted with a single dagger symbol ⸸. Some suggestions fall into the intermediate category and are given the two-dagger status ⸸⸸. Beware of the three-dagger reprisal ⸸⸸⸸. You might end up with the last laugh, but you might be doing your laughing on the unemployment line.

PART ONE
THE QUIZ

THE QUIZ

You may be asking yourself, "Does my boss really deserve this?" Perhaps the answer is yes. Perhaps it is no. Only you can decide if you just want to play a harmless joke, wreak mild havoc on your boss, or embark on a journey of destruction. The following multiple-choice test should help you decide if your boss deserves a ✎ , ✎✎ , or ✎✎✎ rated prank.

1. The first thing my boss insists that I do when I arrive at work in the morning is:

   (a) open the mail
   (b) bring him coffee and a doughnut
   (c) spray his bald spot with Ron Popeil's GLH or some other type of hair in a can

2. Whenever my boss is dieting, she insists I:

   (a) keep plenty of fresh fruit in the fridge
   (b) faithfully praise her efforts
   (c) eat five pounds of chocolate each day and breathe on her constantly

3. When giving dictation, your boss insists on:

   (a) including punctuation
   (b) making you read back each sentence twice
   (c) wearing a crown

4. My boss considers sexual harassment:

   (a) an unpleasant reality of office life
   (b) unfair because it doesn't happen to him often enough
   (c) a "fringe benefit" of my job rather than a crime

5. When my boss attends meetings, she always sits in the back and:

   (a) takes copious notes
   (b) asks important questions
   (c) heckles the speaker

6. Unbeknownst to you, your boss has:

   (a) bragged about your work skills to office mates
   (b) looked through your purse
   (c) raffled off your housecleaning services at various fund-raising auctions on which you must make good

7. Your boss pretends to be a "nice guy" by giving you an extra break every morning. However, he insists you spend this time:

   (a) boning up on your shorthand
   (b) running his personal errands
   (c) massaging his feet

8. You can't prove it, but you know that your boss has stolen:

   (a) an idea from a fellow employee
   (b) a $5 bill from petty cash
   (c) your lunch bag from the fridge more than once

9. You get annoyed when your boss won't return:

   (a) phone calls
   (b) the money he borrowed for lunch
   (c) your red nail polish after he uses it

10. Each year during the holidays, your boss makes you save all the fruitcakes so he/she can:

    (a) donate them to the needy
    (b) bring them to various potluck dinners throughout the year
    (c) give them back next year to the same people who sent them to him/her this year

11. When you're both in a crowd, your boss:

   (a) opens doors for you
   (b) makes you carry his briefcase
   (c) blames any odors he creates on you

12. My boss insists I answer the phone with:

   (a) courtesy
   (b) a pleasant speaking voice
   (c) a Hungarian accent

13. Once a week your boss asks you to spend your lunch hour:

   (a) as his guest for an expensive meal
   (b) picking his children up from nursery school
   (c) performing the Denorex test on him

14. It's unusual for my boss to show up for work:

    (a) late
    (b) with matching socks
    (c) sober

15. My boss usually has more than one:

    (a) meeting scheduled at the same time
    (b) alibi for why he didn't finish his work on time
    (c) mysterious stain on his trousers

16. Coworkers don't like to carpool with my boss because:

    (a) she speeds
    (b) she sings off-key while she drives
    (c) instead of the freeway, she insists on driving on the
        communications super highway

17. Your boss claims the reason he needs you to sit on his lap is:

    (a) none—my boss would never do that
    (b) because he has laryngitis and wants to make sure he
        won't have to strain his voice while giving dictation
    (c) so he can practice his ventriloquist act

18. Your boss always takes vacation the week raises come out
    because:

    (a) she'll have more money to spend on souvenirs for her staff
    (b) she's embarrassed when people thank her for her
        generous raises
    (c) employees can't find her to ask why she lied about
        their raises

19. Every day your boss asks you to take a sip of every beverage he is about to consume. He does this as a:

   (a) gesture of goodwill; what's his is yours
   (b) safeguard against drinking something too hot or cold
   (c) means of having you test-drink his soft drinks in case of contamination

20. On a regular basis, your boss is most likely to open:

   (a) the door for you
   (b) your mail
   (c) his fly

21. Each year during the holidays, your boss starts a Toys for Tots drive in the office. However, you notice he always solicits donations of:

(a) gifts for children under ten years old
(b) gifts for children over ten years old
(c) his favorite brand of alcohol or small power tools

22. Whenever my boss spots me putting something in an envelope, he always asks:

(a) "Do you have enough postage?"
(b) "Are you using company postage for your utility bills?"
(c) "May I lick it?"

23. My boss has been known to spend her lunch hour at:

   (a) the latest seminar learning new achievement skills
   (b) the gym
   (c) the airport Hilton, room 226

24. My boss prides himself on being:

   (a) an upstanding member of society
   (b) able to make it to work after a night on the town
   (c) a Shriner

25. My boss doesn't know the meaning of the word:

   (a) cheap—he's generous to a fault
   (b) thank you—he's not particularly gracious
   (c) homophobe—although he's the biggest one going

26. After returning from a trip to the doctor's office, my boss is likely to say:

   (a) "I'm fit as a fiddle and ready for work"
   (b) "Like I needed to pay that guy sixty-five dollars for him to tell me I need to lose weight!"
   (c) "No more worms!"

27. My boss's breath is so bad that sometimes:

   (a) I have to keep a can of room deodorizer in my desk
   (b) people injure themselves while trying to outrun it
   (c) if she talks long enough, her eyebrows catch on fire!

SCORING

Give yourself one point for every (a) answer, two points for all (b) answers, and three points for (c) answers.

27-40 points

Congratulations! Your boss sounds like a dream and it appears you have nothing to complain about. But don't let that stop you.

41-59 points

Look out! Your boss could go either way, but it's better not to take any chances. Don't let your boss fraternize with other bosses whose bad habits could rub off on him/her. As a matter of fact, keep all contact with the world outside your office to a bare minimum. Don't give phone messages or let him/her see any mail. RSVP "no" to all meetings. Insist everyone he/she tries to reach by phone is not in. This will most likely get your boss fired. But then you will be free to train your new boss to treat you in a manner to which you are more accustomed.

60-81 points

You know the expression "Turn the other cheek"? Well, the only cheek you should show this kind of boss is the one found below your equator. But he or she would probably like that. Whether your boss is an insensitive, Neanderthal brute or an anal-retentive nagger, he/she will never change. And you're not going to change either. But what you can change, thanks to this book, is your boss's relationship with his/her spouse, boss, neighbors, and the IRS.

PART TWO
THE RETALIATION

1 🗡🗡

When your boss's wife calls, pretend you're a temp and don't recognize her voice. Say your boss isn't in the office because he took the afternoon off to spend it with his family.

2 🗡🗡

Have some fun the next time your boss goes on vacation. Call the utility companies and ask that her water and power be turned off until further notice. If they want it in writing, use her letterhead.

3 ⚔⚔⚔

Call your local chapter of the Elvis Presley fan club. Insist Elvis has been showing up on your boss's front lawn at midnight on the tenth of each month. Ask if they can please send authorities out to verify that it is an official Elvis "sighting." Make sure this item appears in all Elvis fan-club newsletters. Even if the officials don't show up, you can bet hundreds of Elvis fans will!

4 🗡️🗡️

Late in the afternoon, remove your boss's car key from his key ring. Wait a few minutes after he leaves for the day, then call security and tell them there is a man (describe your boss) lurking around in the parking lot. Tell the security guard it looked like the man was fondling himself.

5

When the entire office picks names for the Christmas grab bag, tell whoever picks your boss's name that, judging from all the empties you see in her trash can, you know for a fact that your boss would welcome a gift of liquor.

6

Send love poems from your boss to coworkers (male and female!).

7 🗡🗡🗡

If your boss is in the habit of removing his shoes and working in his socks, steal one of the shoes. Claim ignorance and laugh quietly as he leaves work for the day wearing only one shoe. Phase two: Get your hands on some motel letterhead and a bra. Send a letter from the motel to your boss at home (addressed to "Mr. & Mrs.") enclosing some items left behind in haste: his shoe and a bra!

8

Call the IRS as your boss (give her name, address, social security number, etc.) and ask what percentage of people really get caught for tax fraud. Ask what clues they look for to see if someone is cheating on their taxes, then shout, "Hah! I've fooled you five years in a row!" and hang up.

9 🔪🔪

When ordering business cards, get two different styles. Order the regular cards, but order a secret batch for you with an italicized slogan in quotes under your boss's name (e.g., "The Love Doctor" or "The Dominatrix"). Every time your boss sends out correspondence, attach a business card from your private stash.

10

If you have to make all the arrangements for his family vacation, be creative. When dealing with hotels, tell them he would like one large room with roll-away beds so the entire family can sleep together just like at home!

11

Have pride in your boss. Let others know she's been sober for almost two weeks!

12 🔪🔪

If someone accidentally gets locked out of his office at work, offer to pick the lock. Explain that your boss showed you how to break into everyone's office.

13 🔪🔪

Convince your boss's mother that, no matter how much he denies it, he has a life-threatening disease. (Tell her he told you he will always deny this to his mother because he doesn't want to be a burden to her.)

14 🔪🔪

As your boss walks past you on her way out of the office,
jump up and inform her that part of her blouse is not tucked
into her skirt. As you pretend to remedy the situation, take
advantage of the opportunity to affix a stream of toilet paper
to her skirt.

15 🔪🔪

Call accounting and say your boss wants to know whether wager slips from the racetrack qualify as a business expense if the gambling was done during office hours.

16 🔪🔪

The next time your boss's wife calls, ask if she liked the ruby earrings (or some other imaginary gift) your boss asked you to wrap as a gift for her.

17 🔪

Alphabetize her Rolodex by people's *first* names!

18 🔪🔪🔪

Send letters to several retirement villages and convalescent homes in your boss's name. Tell them you're thinking of placing your mother in a home and would like them to send some literature and quotes. Use your boss's mother's address as the return address.

19 🔪🔪

Get the name of the person who has the office directly across the street from your boss's. Call the head of security in your building (as the distraught employee across the street) and complain that every day for the last few weeks someone in the fourth-floor, southwest-corner office is dancing around in his underwear. Tell them you're scared. Ask them to make this man close his drapes or you're going to call the police. When security arrives, tell them that your boss is listening to music and asked "not to be disturbed." Tell them he's been doing that every day for the last two weeks.

20 🗡

Once a week tell your boss that she has a milk "mustache,"
even though you know she doesn't drink milk.

21 🗡🗡🗡

The next time you get an annoying chain letter, fulfill your
karmic duty by sending copies to members of the board of
directors, the legal department, accounting, etc., with your
boss's name on the letter, not yours.

22

After your boss leaves for vacation, let everyone in the office know he did not leave town, he's having cosmetic surgery.

23

Gingerly remove the label from your boss's hairspray can and glue it over a can of yellow spray paint. Then ask coworkers if they saw your boss's bad frosting job.

24

Bring fake dentures or a partial plate to work with you.
Go into the ladies' room right after lunch when it is the
most crowded. Proceed to brush the dentures/partial
plate with a toothbrush in the sink. Let everyone know
you are considering changing jobs because you are tired
of having to clean your boss's teeth!

25

As your boss gets into a crowded elevator,
announce in a loud voice that the proctologist can
see him at three-thirty P.M. about his "rash."

26 🔪🔪🔪

When you see someone going into the ladies' room, sneak in with a coworker. Remove your shoes beforehand so the person in the ladies' room thinks there's only one person coming in. With a whoopee cushion make the foulest of noises several times, then both exit. When the employee exits the ladies' room with a shocked and confused look and asks, "Did you see who just left the ladies' room?" give your boss's name.

27 🔪🔪

Order pizzas to be delivered to you during your boss's four-thirty P.M. meeting. As the delivery person arrives, disappear until he/she gets impatient enough and asks your boss to pay for the pizzas. Your boss will be too embarrassed not to pay for them. When you return to your desk, insist you never ordered any pizzas. You might get a free dinner.

28 🔪

When the big boss comes looking for your boss, say that your boss had a three o'clock appointment with Mr. Golf and Mr. Club (then give him a conspiratorial wink)!

29 🔪🔪

Call the IRS as your boss (give her name, address, social security number, etc.) and ask what percentage of people get audited. Ask how they select the people they audit. Then get mad and say, "Who made you God?"

30 🔪🔪

Give your boss's address to Jehovah's Witnesses and
tell them your boss would like to be visited at home
by one of their missionaries.

31 🗡🗡🗡

If you have a pharmacy in your office building and you know your boss is going there on his way home from work, put a small, previously purchased item (a box of Ex-Lax, condoms, etc.) in his jacket pocket. Secretly follow him into the store and make sure he doesn't see you. Tell security you saw him slip something into his pocket.

32 ///

Your boss and her date are attending an important business-related social function. Rent the male half of a costume (e.g., Raggedy Andy) and send it over to the date's office on the afternoon of the function. In your best "temp" voice, call him and announce that your boss just found out it's a costume party. When he calls your boss to confirm this, inform him that she can't come to the phone; she's having her costume fitted and said she'll meet him at the party. Then let your boss know that her date called and said he can't be reached this afternoon but he'll meet her at the function.

33

Send letters from your boss to all the daytime talk shows—Oprah, Phil, Geraldo, Sally Jessy, et al.—stating that your boss is a Satan-worshiping cross-dresser. The letters should ask if your boss can be included in the next broadcast on that topic. Leave a copy of the letter in your department's busiest Xerox room.

34 ⚔

When his boss calls, announce that your boss has been in the bathroom for the last forty-five minutes.

35 ⚔

Around the holidays, send out gift-wrapped boxes of condoms from your boss to all of her major clients.

36

Call different departments in the company and say your boss has desperately asked you to find some Preparation H.

37

Call your boss's wife's favorite radio station and have a series of songs dedicated to him each day from "The 9 to 5 Club."

38 🔪🔪

Call the health department and make a complaint, in
your boss's name, against one of her next-door neighbors. Report that her neighbors are housing illegal
aliens in their garage, which has no plumbing or heat.
Insist the best time for an inspector to catch them in
the act is after midnight.

39 🔪🔪🔪

Make twenty-five photocopies of your naked rear end. Send them to your boss's closest associates/clients (including your boss's boss!) with a chain letter from your boss. The letter should ask everyone to make copies of their own rear end and send them to five more people. Send a copy to personnel.

40 🔪🔪

Register your boss as a participant in a local charity bachelor auction. Insist all correspondence be sent to his home address, in care of his wife.

41

Register your female boss as a participant in a local charity bachelor auction. When the committee calls to explain they are rejecting her because it needs men whom women will pay to date, let the committee know your boss still wants to be in on the action because (1) most of her dates already pay for her services, and (2) she only dates other women.

42

If the big boss comes looking for your boss between nine and ten A.M., say that your boss is meeting with Regis and Kathie Lee.

43

Start telling your boss's clients/customers that he prefers to be called "Slappy."

44 🔪

When filling out any paperwork for your boss that requires her date of birth, make sure you add "B.C." after the year.

45 🔪

The next time your boss asks you to photocopy any of his or her personal business, make sure to leave a few extra copies in the Xerox machine. This is particularly effective if you are copying tax returns. If your boss yells, yell back that personal business shouldn't be done on company time.

46

Always tell your boss she has lipstick on her teeth.

47

Get some stationery from a hotel your boss stays in
regularly while on business. Use it to send a letter to
your boss's boss from the "manager" stating that
every time your boss frequents the hotel, items
disappear from his or her room.

48

Send letters from him to the A list of clients your firm deals with explaining that he has started his very own customized cape-manufacturing business as a sideline to his existing career. The letter should state that if these clients would like to place an order, he would be more than happy to come over and measure them!

49

Every once in a while, steal the contents of her lunch bag and replace them with a can of Slim-Fast.

50

When setting up a meeting with a potential client, tell the client your boss says wearing pants is optional.

51

Leave a message at your boss's home from the "clinic" saying that he tested negative.

52

When your boss's fiancé calls, compliment him on his exquisite taste in jewelry. Rave about how the rubies in the ring really set off the diamonds. When he protests that the ring doesn't have rubies, apologize and say, "Oh, yeah, the ruby ring was from her last fiancé."

53 🔪

If you have to get your boss's lunch, every once in a while take a bite or two out of it before you deliver it.

54 🔪

Before your boss arrives for an important meeting, let the others know he'll be arriving a tad late because his hemorrhoids have flared up again!

55 🔪

Have an extra hole drilled into your boss's
bowling ball.

56 🔪

When your boss's mother calls, tell her he's in the
bathroom "again."

57 🔪🔪

Bake your boss some chocolate chip cookies. But substitute Ex-Lax for the chocolate chips.

58 🔪

Have pride in your boss. Let others know he hasn't shoplifted in almost three weeks!

59

Add plenty of catnip to her perfume.

60

The next time your boss asks for a cash advance for a business trip, have it converted to Japanese yen.

61

When your boss's wife calls (about one week before their wedding anniversary), greet her with a cheery "Happy anniversary!" When she insists it's not their anniversary, tell her you didn't think so either. Let her know your boss couldn't remember and thought it might be today.

62

Tell your boss that she has a run in her stockings when you know she's not wearing any.

63

Put a frame around your boss's rear license plate with a ridiculous saying (for example, "I'm a virgin and proud of it!"). It might be a while before your boss notices it, but you can rest assured someone will point it out sooner or later.

64

When making his family vacation plans, purchase an extra airline ticket and hotel room for a "Miss Jones." Arrange for all the tickets to be delivered to his home.

65

After your boss has signed some letters to clients, add a hug and kiss ("XO") after her signature.

66

Whistle while you work...nonstop.

67

The next time your boss travels out of town on business, charge the largest fruit basket and a few bottles of the most expensive champagne to his bill and ask that they be waiting for him in his room. Send a fax on company letterhead to the hotel prior to his arrival and ask that it be placed in his room next to the champagne. The fax should have a generic "Congratulations" or "Good luck" greeting from some of his colleagues back at the office. He won't know he's paying for it all until he tries to check out. If he tries to slip it through on his expense account, complain to accounting that his behavior is robbing the company blind.

68

If your boss is meeting with a potential client for the first time, let her know that the client's secretary confidentially told you the client is extremely hard of hearing. The only way he'll hear your boss is if she shouts at him.

69

Call personnel and ask them if the company insurance policy will pay if you get injured by a flying toenail from one of your boss's clip sessions.

70 🔪

Glue a picture of Batman over your boss's passport ID photo.

71 🔪🔪

Right after your boss leaves for the airport, call the airline and report that the tickets issued to your boss were stolen. Give all flight details. Tell them you're not sure, but you think his passport was stolen, too. Remind them if they're not sure who owns the ticket, they can always check the passport photo.

72

When your boss's boyfriend or husband calls, pretend you're a temp and don't recognize his voice. Tell him your boss went to see a psychic to find out when she's going to meet "Mr. Right."

73

If your boss is in the habit of removing her shoes while she works, slip an egg into the toe section while she's not looking.

74

Send a picture of your boss to *Playgirl*. Post the rejection letter in the coffee room.

75

If your boss and her new boyfriend have a date, call her new boyfriend and, in your best "temp" voice, ask him if it's going to be just the two of them or if her children are invited, too. Because if the children are going, they'll need two cars to fit everyone in.

76

Invest in some of those pens whose markings are invisible in the light but "glow in the dark." These will come in handy when you overhear your boss making plans to go to the movies, a concert, or any other event where the lights are turned out. "I'm a sexist pig," "Please kick me," or "For a good time call (*your boss's name and home phone number*)," are just a few of the phrases you can write on your boss's jacket ahead of time without your boss knowing it.

77 🔪

Let whoever needs to know that your boss will be late for the staff meeting because he "soiled" his pants and is having them cleaned.

78 🔪

Call around to a few different offices at work and say that your boss has misplaced her dentures. Ask if anyone has seen them.

79

Place a few boxes of Depend or some other brand
of adult diapers in the supply room and tape a note
to them that reads "Property of
(*your boss's name*)."

80 🔪🔪🔪

The next time you take a European vacation, write out a postcard thanking your boss for paying for the entire trip. Sign his mother-in-law's name and send it to his mother. Ask the desk clerk to mail it a month after you check out to avoid any suspicion.

81

Learn how to throw your voice. This will provide hours of entertainment as you use your newfound skill to get your boss to unknowingly insult strangers in elevators and crowds or make rude and tasteless remarks to clients she wants to impress.

82

Send a "Thinking of you" card in your boss's handwriting to your boss's mother-in-law asking
why it's been so long since
her last visit.

83 🔪🔪

Call the CEO's office and explain that the
cleaning crew said they'd be able to paint over all the
urine stains on your boss's wall, but
they need authorization first.

84 🔪

When your boss's new boyfriend comes to pick her up
at the office, congratulate him on his engagement to
your boss.

85

Come to work early and generously sprinkle some high-potency cow manure around your boss's office. Vacuum it up with a portable vacuum and leave. When you arrive at work at your normal time, insist you don't smell anything odd when your boss asks you. Each time your boss leaves the office, ask other employees if they have some strong air freshener. When they ask "Why?" bring them into your boss's office for a whiff.

86 🔪

Let his female clients/customers/coworkers know your boss always says, "The trouble with this company is that too many women work here instead of staying at home where they belong."

87 🔪

When you enter a crowded elevator and spot your boss's boss, make small talk about how you admire your boss's ability to avoid stress by playing video games on his or her computer all afternoon.

88 🔪

Let whoever needs to know know that your boss will be late for the staff meeting because he's trying to remove the sock that's caught in his pants zipper.

89 🔪

Somehow, let your boss's new boyfriend know that she has started a Lorena Bobbitt fan club.

90

Buy a tube of that new lipstick that's invisible when applied, makes its own color later, then won't wash off for twenty-four hours. Lavishly apply several layers of lipstick to a few tissues. Tell your boss he has something on his face and to stand still so you can remove it. With tissues in both hands, draw some lines across both cheeks and forehead, Indian style. The full color will "bloom" in about ten minutes. Put a clean tissue in your trash can in case your boss wants to see what was on the tissue. This trick is particularly effective on a day when many meetings are scheduled.

91

When your boss's wife calls, say he's taking
another of his "long lunches." (No. 92 works well
with this.)

92

Late in the afternoon, remove your boss's car key from his key ring. Wait a few minutes after he leaves for the day, then follow him down to the garage. After he leaves to call his wife to bring the spare key or pick him up, open the car with the key and strategically place a garter belt, bra, and stockings so they hang out of the trunk and doors and are exposed enough to get his wife's attention as she drives up.

Relock the door.

93 🔪

Just for fun, instead of answering your boss's questions in your normal voice, sing all your responses.

94 🔪🔪

Call the IRS as your boss's wife. Confess that your bookkeeping skills are less than adequate and you're afraid you might be gypping them. Express admiration for their talent and coyly ask if they would consider keeping an eye on all of your boss's future tax returns.

95 🔪

Write to "Love Connection" as your boss asking what she has to do to become a contestant. Post the reply in the Xerox room.

96 🔪

Switch your boss's Sweet 'n Low tablets with Sominex.

97 🔪

When someone in the office gets flowers, sigh and comment
loudly that the only flowers you ever see in your office are
on the bottle of Four Roses whiskey your boss
keeps in his bottom drawer.

98 🔪

If your job includes getting your boss's lunch, be creative. If
she asks for ham and cheese, make sure they use
Limburger cheese.

99

Send a male stripper to the CEO on his birthday as a present from your boss.

100

When someone picks up a pen from your desk and asks if they can borrow it, quickly blurt out, "Don't use that one!" Inform them that you have seen your boss clean his ears, among other body parts, with that pen.

101

Around the holidays, let everyone know that your boss has said about a zillion times that she can't get enough fruitcake!

102

The next time your boss is invited to a meeting, say she wants to know if they're serving alcohol or if it's BYOB.

103 🔪

When your boss's mother calls, tell her he's at the hospital "again."

104 🔪

When the big boss calls, say you promise you'll give your boss the message just as soon as she returns from her job interview.

105 🔪

When your boss's boss calls, take a message. Say that your boss doesn't like to be disturbed during nap time.

106 🔪🔪

Superimpose your boss's picture onto Hulk Hogan's body. Have calendars made up and send it out to clients/customers as a holiday gift from him.

107 🔪🔪

Have a male friend call several doctors pretending to be your female boss's husband. He should explain that his wife has an unusual amount of body hair and has been hinting she'd like heavy-duty electrolysis as a birthday gift. Ask for quotes, availability dates, etc. Let the doctors know that this is not a secret and they have her husband's permission to send all literature to her at work.

108

Before your boss leaves to pick up an important client for lunch or a meeting, run down to the garage and quickly put some big, bright, fluorescent flame decals on the passenger side of the car. Since your boss will be entering the car on the driver's side, the decals won't be noticed. The client might not know your boss well enough to make a joke about the decals and will just assume your boss is a tasteless buffoon.

109 🔪

Update his résumé to include that he freelances as Ronald McDonald on weekends without pay or permission.

110 🔪🔪

Get your hands on a few embarrassing pictures of your boss (sunbathing during last year's vacation, at the company Christmas party, or superimpose your boss's face over a compromising photo) and have them turned into slides. The next time your boss is giving a slide presentation, slip a few of your slides in with the work slides.

111

Have a male friend pretend to be your boss and call several insurance companies. He should tell them that he's considering taking out a million-dollar life-insurance policy on his wife and that it's okay to call his home during the day and leave the quotes with his wife.

112

If you work for a doctor, the next time there's a
waiting room full of patients, let them know that
the doctor is still meeting with the attorneys about
all of the doctor's pending
malpractice suits.

113 🔪🔪

If you know your boss had dinner at his boss's house last night, take a message when the big boss calls. Let the big boss know that your boss spent most of the morning in the bathroom getting rid of some swill he said he ate last night.

114 🔪

If your boss's weight is under two hundred, change the weight on his driver's license from "1__" to "4__."

115 🔪🔪🔪

When you know your boss is taking his wife out to dinner,
find out where and go to the same restaurant. Have your
boss paged to take a phone call, giving him a reason to leave
the table. A few minutes after he returns, give the waiter a
note to be delivered to your boss's wife and have the waiter
tell her, "The woman across the room says she's not interested and asked that this note be returned to this table."
Leave quickly. The note should be suggestive
and should also be in your boss's
forged handwriting.

116 ///

When you know your boss is taking his boss out to lunch,
find out where and go to the same restaurant. Have your
boss paged to take a phone call, giving him a reason to leave
the table. A few minutes after he returns, give the waiter a
note to be delivered to your boss's boss and have the waiter
tell him, "The man across the room says he's not interested
and asked that this note be returned to this table." Leave
quickly. The note should be suggestive and should also be in
your boss's forged handwriting.

117 🔪

When you and your boss are alone and out of earshot of any
witnesses, repeat everything you say twice
just to annoy him.

118 🔪🔪🔪

If your boss has too much to drink at some office function
and passes out, drive him home and leave him on the porch.
It's more fun for everyone if it's not his actual home.

119 🔪🔪🔪

Whenever you witness a hit-and-run accident, place a note on
the windshield of the hit car identifying your boss as the driver of the other vehicle. The note should say that your boss
is more than glad to pay for any damage. Make sure you
include both your boss's home and work phone numbers.

120 🔪

Have pride in your boss! Let her new boyfriend know
that she just lost a total of two hundred pounds, for
the third time!

121 🔪

If someone comments that your boss looks like he's
gaining weight, tell them it's just that his
colostomy bag is full.

122 🔪

When reading back dictation or delivering an
important message, lip-sync
every fourth word.

123

If your boss has a formal function to attend and plans on changing at work in order to save time, call a second tux shop and have an extra pair of shoes, size 13 EEE, delivered. When the real tux and shoes are delivered, your boss will probably slip on the tux jacket and check that the shoes are the right size. Once he is satisfied that everything is okay, substitute the size 13 EEE shoes for the size 10s.

124 🔪

When no one is looking, place a potato in your boss's exhaust pipe. This is particularly effective when it's crucial that your boss be somewhere in a hurry.

125 🔪

Whenever your boss says, "Where've you been all my life?" remind him that for his first thirty years, you weren't born yet.

126 🔪

Buy some sleazy teen fan-club or soft-porn magazines and place a mailing sticker on them to show your boss as the subscriber. Leave them in the coffee room.

127 🔪

When your boss's wife calls, ask if she's his first or second wife.

128 🔪🔪

When making dental appointments for your boss, mention to the dentist's office staff that she's on medication and her physician insists that novocaine be avoided at all costs.

129 🔪🔪

Have your boss's car towed while she's at the dentist.

130 🔪

When clients arrive for a meeting, assure them your boss
won't be long. Tell them he's just making a quick
call to his bookie!

131 🔪🔪

When arranging business trips that include long flights with
more than one meal, make sure the airline knows that your
boss adheres to a strict diet. Insist that due to religious
reasons, he can only eat cold oatmeal.

132 🔪🔪

The day before your boss returns from vacation, open all the windows to her office and sprinkle birdseed everywhere. After all the pigeons eat and relieve themselves, help them find their way back outside, close up the windows, and get rid of any extra bird-seed. You will, of course, claim to have no knowledge of why there are large amounts of birdshit all over her office.

133

Ask a coworker ahead of time to call you when she sees you're about to take dictation. Answer the phone in your boss's office. Listen for an appropriate amount of time, then reply, "I'm sorry, but I wasn't here during lunch yesterday when the CEO and the 'new guy' were measuring Mr. (*your boss's name*)'s office." When your boss is finally able to speak and asks who was on the phone, tell him it was a contractor who said he left something here yesterday. Be vague.

134 🔪

When leaving your boss's phone number on someone's
answering machine, remember to speak clearly, slowly, and
to throw in an extra digit or two.

135 🔪

The next time your boss goes on vacation, tell everyone he
went to the Elvis-impersonator
convention in Vegas.

136 //

It's important to keep your boss's desk and work area neat.
Whatever can't be finished in eight hours
should be thrown out.

137 ///

When your boss asks you to wrap a gift of clothing for his
wife, tape a note inside that reads: "Thanks (*your boss's
name*). This is lovely, but it's way too large for me.
Maybe your wife can use it."

138 🔪🔪🔪

When sending paperwork to your boss's boss,
"accidentally" attach a copy of a memo from
your boss to another coworker asking if he/she
heard whether or not this year's raises were
going to be better than last year's or if
the boss was going to continue
to be a skinflint.

139 🔪

When someone compliments your new scarf, tell them your boss made it. Confidentially tell them he learned to knit and crochet while he was in rehab.

140 🔪

Buy a "Good Luck" card for your boss and pass it around the office for everyone to sign. Attach a note explaining the good wishes are for his audition in the male-spokesmodel category on "Star Search."

141

Sing "New York, New York" at the top of your
lungs each time your boss mentions
that city while dictating.

142

When your boss's mother calls, tell her he went
to see the priest again.

143 🔪

Empty the hand-lotion and/or soap bottles in your boss's
office bathroom and refill them
with mayonnaise.

144 🔪🔪

Fill one of the holes in his bowling ball with
liquid cement.

145

Have a rubber stamp made that reads, "I need to be spanked." Stamp this next to your boss's signature on all outgoing correspondence before mailing it.

146

The next time your boss is out of the office for a few days and people ask if he's sick, let them know he's having a breast-reduction operation. This works well if your boss is hefty.

147

If your boss has been elected to hire the
waitresses/bartenders for an important
work-related social function,
make sure you hire them
from a topless agency.

148 🔪🔪

If your boss hosts lunch meetings and orders food in, the next time you're serving up Chinese food in front of his clients or associates announce, "The restaurant said they can't prepare your favorite, sweet-and-sour dog, without at least twenty-four hours notice."

149

Write a letter from your boss to Warner Bros.
asking permission to borrow the Batmobile.
Then accidentally leave the
rejection letter in
the Xerox room.

150 🔪🔪

Put some lipstick on, blot it onto a sheet of white paper, and
cut out the outline of your lips. Use the paper as a
pattern to trace your lips onto a thin sponge
and cut out. Apply lipstick to the sponge.
As you stand behind your boss waiting for
him to sign something, very gently
press the sponge onto his
shirt collar.

151 ✂✂

Ask all females who enter your office to divulge their mea-
surements. When they ask why, tell them that your boss has
a hobby of trying to guess everyone's bra size.

152 🔪

If, when you're setting up an important business lunch, the
client wants to pick the restaurant, let him/her know that,
although management decided not to press charges, your
boss is no longer welcome at the Sizzler.

153 🗡

If your boss makes you take his clothes to the cleaners, every once in a while make sure you ask for triple extra starch.

154 🗡

Have pride in your boss. Let others know he hasn't asked to wear any of your clothing in the last week!

155 🔪

Paint fake eyeballs on your boss's
eyeglasses.

156 🔪

Start telling his clients/customers he prefers to
be called by his gang name "C.E. Yo-yo," "Ice
President," or "Corporate Cube."

157

Call the FBI and let them know you have
repeatedly overheard your boss make
inquiries about where to purchase
explosive devices.

158

Let your boss know you're studying to be a street mime.
Once a week, mime all of your boss's phone messages as if
you're in a wind tunnel.

159

When meeting his wife/girlfriend for the first time, say, "Oh,
I didn't realize you were a brunette. The woman in the
picture on his desk is a blonde."

160 🔪

Ask the CEO's secretary how much it would cost to insulate
your boss's office. Tell her people are complaining
about the loud snoring.

161 🔪

When RSVPing to a work-related evening social function,
leave word that your boss will not be in attendance because
that's the night he takes his weekly bath.

162 ⚔

Make a bumper sticker out of nonremovable contact paper and place it on your boss's rear bumper. It should read: "Honk if you want to see me naked. Honk twice if you don't!"

163 ⚔

When anyone asks how your boss met and married his wife, tell them he said they met in a bar and it was cheaper to marry her than keep on paying her hourly rates.

164

Cancel meetings for two consecutive days each month. Simply inform whomever you're canceling that it's not a good idea for your boss to be seen in public during a full moon.

165

The next time your boss is out of the office for a few days
and people ask if he's sick, let them know he's having his
buttocks enhanced. This works well if your boss is slight.

166

Steal the remote control from your boss's home television.
On Super Bowl Sunday or some other big sports day, hide in
the bushes outside his house and
switch channels every five minutes.

167

Start wearing fishnet stockings and
stiletto pumps to the office. When
people question the decline of your
taste, insist your boss is
making you wear them.

168

If you are invited to your boss's house to watch family vacation/wedding/bar-mitzvah videos, bring a universal remote and hide it in your pocket. As soon as you get bored, turn the power off. Repeat until your boss gets so frustrated he or she decides not to show the movies anymore.

169 🔪

Call your boss a son of a bitch. When his veins pop, say, "I was acting! I'm good, aren't I?"

170 🔪

During the holiday season, sprinkle Styrofoam chips all over your boss's office. Then tell her it snowed.

171 🗡🗡🗡

When your boss is attending an out-of-town convention or meeting in another city without his wife, have a friend of yours call his house when you know his wife will be the only one answering the phone. Your friend should pretend to be the reservations clerk at a posh hotel in the convention city. The reason for the call is to tell Mr. and Mrs. (*fill in your boss's name*) the good news that, due to a cancellation, your boss's name cleared the waiting list for the honeymoon suite. The dates your friend confirms should be the exact dates your boss is attending the convention.

172 🔪

After you take your boss's car to be washed, affix "delivery" decals to the car doors and glue a large plastic bucket of chicken to the roof.

173 🔪🔪

When your boss's wife calls, pretend you're a temp and don't recognize her voice. Say your boss isn't in the office because he's having his free consultation with the divorce lawyer.

174 🔪🔪

If your boss has too much to drink at some office function and passes out, have coworkers help you bring her back to her office. Then apply a dozen press-on tattoos to various limbs.

175 🔪🔪

When your boss is late for an important meeting, let whoever is waiting for him know he's still at the peep show... performing.

176

Just for fun, each day use a word that does-n't mean anything as part of your boss's phone message. For example: "Mr. Jones would like you to give him a quote on the latest lupash!"

177

Call all of your boss's old girlfriends and tell
them he's available again. Give them his
home number and address. Tell them
it's not necessary to call
before dropping by.

178 🔪🔪

At Christmas, make up an official-looking gift certificate on your computer from your boss to his boss, which states that for one year your boss is going to either hand-wash his boss's car or mow his lawn, whichever his boss prefers. When his boss calls in his preference, your boss will be too embarrassed not to go along with it.

179

When your boss's mother calls, tell her he went to his lawyer's office to make out his will.

180

Put a suggestion in the suggestion box in your boss's name that it's high time a vending machine for condoms was installed in the men's room.

181 🔪🔪🔪

Have a male friend pretending to be your boss
call several plastic surgeons. He should explain that his wife
asked him to give her as a birthday present a much-needed
head-to-toe cosmetic overhaul. They should
send the brochures directly to his wife.
Give your boss's wife's
name and address.

182 🔪

Set up an appointment for your boss to make a donation with the local sperm bank. Ask them to confirm in writing to his home address.

183 🔪

If anyone comments on what a nice couple your boss and her husband make, agree. Tell them that it must have been fate they were both appearing on "Geraldo" that day.

184 🔪🔪

Have a male friend call the IRS as your boss
(give his name, address, social security number, etc.) and ask if the cruise he and his wife
took last year to Barbados can be a business
write-off because he absentmindedly packed his
briefcase and took work with him by mistake.

185 🔪

Help coworkers come to the conclusion that your boss was one of the Village People. Get one of their old albums, write an inscription to a fan on it in your boss's signature, then leave it in the coffee room. If anyone questions his resemblance, remind them it was almost twenty years ago.

186 🔪

Have pride in your boss! Let others know she's the only member of her family who hasn't been incarcerated!

187

Take an ad out in *Soldier of Fortune* magazine in
your boss's name for a huge garage sale at her house
to unload surplus ammunition, machetes, bayonets,
and sawed-off shotguns. Make sure you include
the phrase "The earlier you show up, the
bigger the discount!"

188

Have a friend call the CEO's office pretending to
be a delivery person waiting in the lobby. He
should state that security needs an okay before
he can deliver the bed your boss
ordered for his office.

189

When your boss calls in sick, let her boss know that she
won't be in for a day or two. Without missing a beat, ask
if someone can recommend a good
bail-bond service.

190

When your boss is not looking, glue a few dozen brightly
colored toothpicks on the top of his shoes.

191

Give your boss's mother-in-law a complete vacation itinerary.
Make sure you include addresses, phone and fax numbers.
Let it "slip" that he secretly wished she might
join his family on vacation.

192

Send a memo from your boss to personnel trying to initiate
"Bikini Day" at the office.

193 🗡️🗡️

When your boss is attending an out-of-the-office meeting, call ahead of time and ask that a calculator be placed close to where your boss will be sitting. Confidentially let them know that your boss usually counts on his fingers and has trouble with numbers greater than ten.

194 🗡🗡

Every year, send a Father's Day card to your boss's house from "Junior." "Junior" should write in the card that he looks forward to meeting his dad's "other" family someday soon.

195 🗡🗡

If your boss makes you do all of her holiday shopping, charge a gift for yourself each time you charge a gift for her.

196

Keep copies of your boss's monthly expense report after he signs it. Then add a few extra entries like the receipt for your new dishwasher. White-out your name and address on the receipt and type in his. Put this in the "miscellaneous" column, list it as a "gift," then wait for accounting to contact him. You, of course, will have a copy of the real expense report on file. When you compare your version with the one accounting rejected, you might suggest that someone in the company is out to "get" him.

197

The next time you make airline reservations for your boss, say he wants to know if he can get double mileage on his frequent-flier account, the reason being that he insists he's a vessel for our Lord and that means, technically, there are two of them flying. Then ask the airline to keep a very close eye on him during the flight.

198

When arranging a meeting at a client's office, ask if the meeting can be held as close as possible to a bathroom. Confidentially, let the person on the other end of the phone know that since your boss started on his "medication," he just doesn't have the same control he used to.

199

When someone calls for your boss right after lunch,
inform them that she's in the ladies' room brushing
her tooth. When they ask, "Don't you mean 'teeth'?,"
tell them she already cleaned her dentures, now
she's brushing her "real" tooth.

200

When your boss's wife calls, don't put her through. In your best "temp" voice, explain that he told you he's been a widower for years. Just for fun, add, "He couldn't possibly have a wife, or he wouldn't be taking me out to dinner tonight." Later on, call your boss's wife and say your boss has to work late.

201

When his mother calls, tell her he went to look at cemetery plots.